S0-CPS-818

Dear Parent,

In <u>What Is a Star?</u> your child will learn why stars twinkle and which star can be seen during the daytime. Wise Mrs. Owl tells Christoper how stars grow bigger and brighter. She even tells him how many stars there are in the sky. Can you guess the number? Turn the page to find out if you are right.

Sincerely,

Rita D. Gould

Managing Editor

FAMILY FUN

- In the early evening, go outside with your child to look at the stars. Locate the Big Dipper, the Little Dipper, and the North Star for your child.

- Make a nighttime star picture. Using blue, purple, red, and yellow crayons, help your child color the entire surface of a piece of white paper. Then with a black crayon, color over this colored background. With a blunt object, scratch away the black crayon with your child to reveal many "stars." Add a moon or other objects to the picture.

READ MORE ABOUT IT

- *What Makes Day and Night?*
- *What Is the Moon?*

WEEKLY READER BOOKS presents

What Is a Star?

A **Just Ask**™ Book

Hi, my name is Christopher!

by Chris Arvetis
and Carole Palmer

illustrated by
James Buckley

FIELD PUBLICATIONS
MIDDLETOWN, CT.

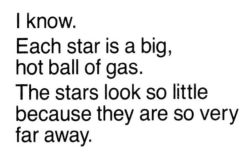

I know.
Each star is a big,
hot ball of gas.
The stars look so little
because they are so very
far away.

She knows!

One shiny star we know
is the sun.
It is closer to us than
any other star.
That's why it shines so
bright and looks so big.

All the stars shine
day and night.
When the sun is out, it is
so bright we cannot see
the light of other stars.

No one knows how stars begin.
Scientists think that whirling dust and gas in space form the stars.
They grow bigger and bigger as they whirl like tops.

The star becomes hotter
and hotter as it grows.
The heat makes the glow
that lights up the sky.

SUPERGIANT

GIANT

Stars are far away.
The sun is millions
of miles away.
The star nearest the sun
is many millions of miles
farther away.
That's why stars look
so little.

Starlight comes in many colors.
Look at the colors stars can be.
The hottest stars have a bluish-purple color.
The coolest are a red color.
The sun is yellow in color—halfway between the hottest and coolest.

The starlight shines through the air around the earth.
That air is moving.
The way it moves makes the starlight blink on and off.
That's why stars look like they twinkle.

BIG DIPPER

LITTLE DIPPER

NORTH STAR

Within The Milky Way, stars are part of smaller groups called constellations.
Look at the North Star and the constellations Big Dipper and Little Dipper.